THE GOOD DOG FOOD GUIDE

ROSEMARY AND ANDREW GASSON
ILLUSTRATED BY ROBIN RAY

Chatto & Windus
LONDON

AUTHORS' NOTE

All the foods tested here are of the high quality required of Dog Food. This is a guide to taste, and other useful information such as packaging, availability, etc. The Dog Foods in our Reports have, where possible, been tested by several dogs, and ratings given by experienced dog owners according to our Wet Nose rating system (p. 27). Where scores differed, we have taken an average; where scores differed dramatically we have re-tested. The Ratings and Human comments are made by dog owners who know their dogs well and understand their reactions.

Published 1993 by
Chatto & Windus Ltd
20 Vauxhall Bridge Road
London SW1V 2SA

A CIP catalogue record for this book is
available from the British Library

ISBN 0 7011 4873 X

Photoset by Selwood Systems, Midsomer Norton
Printed in Great Britain by
Butler & Tanner Ltd, Frome, Somerset

ACKNOWLEDGEMENTS

INTERWOOF AGENTS
Len Allen
Robert Albertson
Michael & Marianne Barnett
Patricia Bernie
Peter Bluff
Francois Bringer
Andrew Day
Martin Day
Jeffery & Rosalind Dobkin
Carolyn Dover
Ruth Forder
Rowland Fowles
Michael Gavshon
Sharon Glover
Gabriele Hemken
Kurt Hoefle
Varda Lemare
Jaques Meringhi
Shona Niven
Paola Pasquini
Anthony Phillips
David Randall
Max Savage
Simone Schweinitz
Douglas Sefton
Jill Smith
Andrew Stevenson
Alan Sweet
Martha Teichner
Sydney Trattner
Nicholas Turner
Ian Valvona
Lisa Wolfe

HONORARY INSPECTORS
Bruno from Wethersfield
Cindy from Stanmore
Miffy from Hampstead
Twiglet the three-legged whippet from
Beoley

CANINE FOOD PURVEYORS
Armitage Pet Products
Asda Stores
Edward Baker
Beta Petfoods
Budgens Stores
Continental Canners
Creg Vetfoods
Cycle Advance Nutrition
Denes Natural Petcare
Friskies Petcare
Gateway Foodmarkets
Gilbertson & Page
Hall Harrison Cowley
Hill's Pet Products
Kingfisher Premier Foods
Leander International
Marks & Spencer
Midland Petfood Canners
Paragon Petcare
Pascoe's Pet Products
Peak Dog Foods
Pedigree Petfoods
Pets Choice
Quaker UK
Ralston Purina International
Repnor Gold Products
Royal Canin
Safeway Supermarkets
Sainsbury's Supermarkets
Spillers Foods
Tesco Stores
Thomas's Europe
Town & Country Petfoods
Wafcol Vegetarian Foods
Wagg Foods
Waitrose Supermarkets
Wundpets

OTHERS
James Allcock BVSc. M.R.C.V.S.
PFMA

The dog food must get through...

This Guide remains independent in its editorial selection and does not accept advertising or payment from any dog food manufacturers.

All the foods mentioned in this Guide have been **genuinely tested by real dogs**. All information was correct at the time of testing for brand name, flavour, pack size etc, and was taken from the labels or manufacturers' fact sheets.

Seriously.

A FEW WORDS
OF INTRODUCTION

FROM MONTY, THE CHIEF INSPECTOR

Welcome to the *Good Dog Food Guide!* The following reports present interesting new Dog Foods as well as many old favourites. There is something for everyone, whether you're an Irish Wolfhound on a health diet, or a miniature poodle with a penchant for 'postman tartare'.

Research and testing are carried out by two groups of dedicated Canine Inspectors – eight full-time professionals with multi-purpose taste buds, and six part-time Auxiliaries with specialised age or health requirements. All are trained to achieve common standards of judgement with as much objectivity as the field allows, assisted by radio-controlled collars, electronic leads and other modern technology.

Our test methods are simple and designed to emulate the Canine consumer. We randomly allocate to each Inspector a representative selection of food types from both large and small manufacturers. Each food is tasted and rated on our 'Wet Nose' Scale from 1–5. In the event of disagreement, as Chief Inspector I adjudicate.

The entries are listed in alphabetical order of brand name, or occasionally of manufacturer. The Editors have taken DFI Training Courses in Dog Food Identification and are trained to sniff out the very best in new and adventurous eating. They have also decided that it's a dog's life being a Human carrying home 20kg sacks of dry food.

The following pages are intended to give our Canine subscribers an idea of the food fare currently available, plus a few tips on healthy eating. Meanwhile, our investigations continue. . . .

MONTY
(Chief Inspector)

Food ~~War~~ games.

I'm a three year old black and white Cocker Spaniel, reporting for duty at 35lbs. My real name is Montgomery but the other Inspectors call me the General – I'm the only one who can bring some discipline to these troops of mine. 'Eatership by example' is my motto! I have two billets, one in Battersea (close to the you-know-where) during weekdays; and the other in Oxfordshire at weekends for 'War Games'. These involve cross-country manoeuvres looking for the enemy disguised as rabbits and squirrels. The only trouble is that with civilians I find it hard to distinguish between friend and foe and very often end up in solitary, confined to barracks by my Human for behaviour unbecoming an Officer and a Canine. I call him the Collar Sergeant, though, so that I can pull rank.

Favourite food: Denes Healthmeal Natural White Meat; and Spillers Mini Chops.

Hobbies: Chewing army property to matchwood.

Unusual eating: Against regulations, but I do occasionally raid my Human's mess tin when he's not looking.

PIGGY
(Deputy Chief Inspector)

My public recognise me as the thespian 'ham' of the team but can't decide whether they prefer me as Lassie or Rin Tin Tin. I'm five years old, only knee high but exceedingly wide for a black, white and tan English Bull Terrier at an over-indulged 82lbs. I live in Sloane Square and love to be pampered so it's fortunate that I have my own *au pair*. She panders to my every bark and looks after all my needs. Especially when my Human is away, she walks, feeds and keeps me company. I am also very clothes conscious and adore my red polo neck sweater, hand-knitted in Albania, and my Burberry raincoat for inclement weather.

Favourite food: Hill's Science Diet Maintenance Dry.

Hobbies: Over-acting in front of the fridge. raiding dustbins for leftovers; and chasing smaller Canines in the park.

Unusual eating: Oranges and onions (not together).

BELLA

The other Inspectors call me Bella The Bitch but they have to keep me on because they know I'm a fine judge of gourmet food. I'm a colour-coordinated Alsatian with good legs and a great body. My weight is an aerobically perfect 51lbs and I'm usually seen wearing a low-cut diamond-studded collar. Eat your heart out, Joan Collins!

I live in trendy Hampstead with my Human who is now well trained to do exactly what I want. I make his life miserable if he doesn't or have a fling with a passing stranger to make him jealous. You can meet some famous dogs up on the Heath and I like to show him off as my 'toy-boy'.

Favourite food: Hi Life Gourmet Beef, Vegetables & Brown Rice; Spillers Goodlife Chicken & Liver.

Hobbies: Driving around in an open sports car; or slumming it.

Unusual eating: Sirloin steak and bourbon biscuits.

CLEO & TASHA

We are the Twins, Tasha the Dachshund and Cleo the Dachshund-on-stilts (well a Dobermann really) but what's a 50lb difference in weight between sisters. Cleo pretends to be in charge because she's the 'heavy' but the truth is she's a big softie. Her bark is a lot worse than her bite – give her a treat and she's anybody's. Tasha may be small but she's actually the 'boss' and barks the orders – legs aren't everything you know. Still, our black and tan colouring is identical, nobody can tell us apart and we both enjoy the same sort of food. We also like to chase the next door feline. One of us goes for the feet and the other for the head; we haven't caught him yet as we're not quite coordinated.

Favourite food: Safeway Reward Rabbit flavour.

Hobbies: Digging and re-landscaping gardens.

Unusual eating: Spaghetti and bananas.

CRACKERS

I'm retired now, a black, brown and white sheepdog from Manchester. I'm really very large but pride myself on not being overweight, taking my Human for a long walk every afternoon. My days of active chasing are over, but I still remember the good old times when I was in charge and had to round up the sheep. Nowadays, I'm happy to put my paws up and count them instead. If I wake up with a snore and a start, I've probably miscounted and have to begin all over again.

Favourite food: Kennomeat Original; Cycle Senior.

Hobbies: Watching 'One Dog and his Man' on TV and supervising amateur sheep racing.

Unusual eating: Ice cream, and large bones from the butcher.

DOUGAL

No, I've never been on a roundabout in my life. I'm Dougal the cricketer who runs like a googly because the legs are all different – one short, one square, one long and one at least very fine. It's all due to my rather confused ancestry and because my human's a leather on willow fanatic. My beige and brown coat is in team colours and I help out on the village green near Tunbridge Wells as honorary twelfth dog. I can distract the opposition, water the pitch to create a sticky wicket or bark an appeal. I prefer to help the tail enders but have to watch out in case the umpire strikes back. We also like to listen to Test Match Special – I call it Test Munch Special because if they're not eating then I am.

Favourite food: Bounce Lamb (and Turkey); Winalot Wholegrain.

Hobbies: Fast bowling and ambulance chasing.

Unusual eating: Anything round like Maltesers or marshmallows.

DUKE

I always wanted to be a sniffer dog. They said that despite brown and white markings flyweight Jack Russells with short legs were too small to work at Heathrow, let alone commute from King's Lynn every day. I told them I definitely had 'the Nose' and was so well endowed that the rest of the team called me Cyrano. So it's private enterprise instead, sniffing out everything from lamb chops at twenty paws to last week's buried treasure. I live with a rather snooty Feline and regularly inspect and confiscate her lunch. Raiding keeps me in good practice and I might well re-apply for a job with the 'Dug' Squad.

Favourite food: Cesar Select Menus Turkey & Lamb; and Beef & Marrowbone Minced Morsels.

Hobbies: Food sniffing and ball control with 'the Nose'.

Unusual eating: Rice pudding and chicken livers.

Duke.

RAMBO

I'm a fighter, so they call me Rambo. I was rescued from the back ledge of a Ford Cortina where I was a 'Noddy Dog'. There's no reason why a Yorkshire Terrier from Leeds shouldn't be a security guard and I can do a passable imitation of a Rottweiler. At 15lbs I'll take on any instep in town - and I can growl with a Northern accent. Don't tell the enemy but my weak spot is rabbits. I had a bad experience when young which the shrink says explains my bunny phobia - I can't even eat it.

Favourite food: Spillers Prime Turkey flavour; Buffet à la Carte, Game.

Hobbies: Unmentionable.

Unusual eating: Cheese and Rich Tea biscuits.

AUXILIARY INSPECTORS

Our Auxiliary Inspectors were responsible for evaluating the food testings in their own specialist areas

BENJI

Senior/Less Active Food Specialist.
Breed: Miscellaneous.
Age: 11 Years.
Favourite food: Hill's Science Diet, Canine Senior.

BENSON JR

Puppy/Junior Food Specialist.
Breed: Corgi (No relation to you know who....)
Age: 1 Year.
Favourite food: Pedigree Chum Puppy Food.

DAISY

Health Food Specialist (Including Medical & Vegetarian products both wet and dry).
Breed: Dachshund.
Age: 9 Years (... but she lies about her age).
Favourite food: Hill's Prescription Diet (I/D).

See pp. 118-20 for Specialist Food Testings and Suggesting Eating

TAMMY

Dry Food Specialist.
Breed: Dalmatian.
Age: 4 Years.
Favourite Food: Hardy Complete.

GEMMA

'Limited Editions' Specialist.
(We use the phrase 'Limited Editions' to describe
wet dog food ranges that were either produced by
the smaller independent manufacturers, consisted
of only one brand, or had only a few flavours.)
Breed: Bassett Hound.
Age: 5 Years.
Favourite food: Nisa Dogfood – Rabbit.

TERRY

'Limited Editions' Specialist.
Breed: Australian Terrier.
Age: 4 Years.
Favourite food: Tex Chunks – Chicken & Tripe.

See pp. 118–20 for Specialist Food Testings and Suggested Eating

FIDO FACT FILE

SOME DEFINITIONS

Complete Foods contain all the nutrients necessary for good health, except water. They are precisely balanced in the correct proportions by the manufacturer. Be careful not to upset this balance with unnecessary and expensive supplements.

Complementary Foods do not on their own include all the necessary ingredients and must be fed in conjunction with other foods.
e.g. a **Complementary** canned food may be formulated to be served with a **mixer** or **meal**. A **mixer** is therefore not just for bulk but is an essential part of a nutritionally balanced diet. Canned food and mixer must be used in the correct proportions which could be either by weight or volume according to the manufacturer's recommendations.

Always read the labels carefully and remember that different foods from the same manufacturer could be either Complete or Complementary.

Chews, chomps, Human food and titbits are all **Complementary**.

Flavour, Variety, Recipe and **With** do not have the strict legal definitions of Human food in the UK. Good manufacturers include a substantial quantity of the named ingredient although it would be possible for this to be present as quite a small percentage.

A GOOD DIET

Always read the instructions on the label or packet – TWICE

Use a clean feeding bowl which won't tip over, put it in a quiet place and don't disturb while eating.

Food should be warmish – body temperature is best – not straight from the fridge.

If in doubt about your Canine's nutrition, consult a vet. Look out for diarrhoea or constipation; loss of weight or poor appetite; overeating or obesity; wind or halitosis!

Overeating is the main cause of overweight Canines. There is greater risk of cardiac, respiratory or joint disorders. More of a problem with age, females, neutered Canines – and overweight owners!

A good diet should be palatable and include Proteins, Carbohydrates, Fats, Vitamins and Minerals – all in the correct proportions to maintain good health.

Canines cannot be fed on meat alone or they would suffer from vitamin and mineral deficiencies. In the wild, they would eat all the unmentionable bits including the prey's stomach which contains vegetable matter.

Cooked fish with NO bones can be a substitute for meat.

CHANGING TO A NEW DIET

Sudden change in diet (e.g. wet to dry, or even from one brand of wet to another) may give digestive upsets such as diarrhoea, constipation or wind.

Introduce over a 5–10 day period.

Mix the new diet with the previous type, gradually increasing the proportion.

Sometimes hand feed the new diet for a few days.

Possibly mix a dry food with a small amount of water (according to instructions on the label) and wait 10 minutes before serving.

FEEDS

Do not determine size of feed by size of feeding bowl – read the labels.

Decide according to age, size, activity and temperament.

Don't choose food solely on basis of price and packaging.

Feed at a regular time, usually once a day.

But some Canines may be better fed twice a day, including working dogs (require 50% more energy than retired Canines); and some small dogs with a relatively high energy consumption.

Serve about one-third of daily intake at breakfast. This can be as a Crunch. Serve the main meal with warm water to soak and soften before eating.

Giant breeds and some senior Canines may need 2-4 smaller meals a day, to avoid straining their digestive systems.

Crunchy food exercises teeth and gums and helps prevent tartar.

Bones are not essential to the diet and some vets advise against them in case they splinter. Certainly **avoid** small bones such as chicken or rabbit (they become more brittle on cooking).

Avoid sugar, sweets, cake, etc, to help prevent obesity.

Chocolate in dog treats and snacks is specially formulated for the Canine diet and is different from Human chocolate.

Always ensure there is an adequate supply of drinking water available.

Yum.

JUNIOR CANINES

Because they are growing, puppies need more energy than the same sized adult Canine. Feed little and often - 3 or 4 meals per day for the first 14 weeks.

Use bite-size nuggets or soak well.

Growth or **Puppy** foods contain extra vitamins and minerals so it is not necessary to add extra.

Hiccups often come from bolting food.

Growth occurs until 8-14 months, depending on breed.

Growth foods may be more concentrated - avoid excess.

SENIOR CANINES

Depending on breed and age, senior Canines may need:

Fewer calories to avoid obesity.

Less but high quality protein for kidney health.

Increased fibre.

Reduced sodium and phosphorus.

Feeding more often, 2–4 times a day, with small meals providing extra 'high spots' during the day.

HEALTHY EATING & SPECIAL DIETS

There is now a wide choice of foods for healthy eating or other special diets.

Light ('Lite') Foods for overweight Canines, or adult dogs with low activity levels. They have lower calorie levels with some of the fats replaced by carbohydrates.

Do not feed Light Foods to puppies, pregnant or nursing females, or working dogs.

Vegetarian Foods. Most consider that Canines, because of their teeth and digestive system, are best suited to a meat diet. However, there may be occasional instances where a proper vegetarian diet could be beneficial. Vegetables and cereals should be cooked. Extruded manufactured foods are cooked under pressure for maximum digestibility.

Performance, **Activity** or **Racing Foods** for working or sporting Canines, with high protein content to give extra energy.

Small Breed for small-sized adults with high metabolism but low digestive capacity.

Natural with no artificial colourings, flavourings or preservatives.

Gluten Free for Canines with wheat or gluten allergy.

Soya Free with no soya protein which some Canines find difficult to digest.

MEDICAL OR PRESCRIPTION DIETS

There are also several **veterinary foods** available for particular medical conditions, as below.

These are obtainable only on prescription from vets and must be fed in accordance with their instructions.

Food allergies – selected protein diets.

Kidney problems – low or medium protein diets.

Digestive disorders – low fat formulations.

Heart disease – low salt formulation, supplemented with extra B-Group vitamins.

Diabetes

FOOD TYPES

WET FOOD *(Canned)*

Practical

Stores well until opened

Tasty

Nutritious

Retains the moisture content of the basic ingredients which may, like raw meat, consist of up to 80% water

May be either Complete or Complementary

May be formulated for specialised age or health requirements

SEMI-MOIST

Convenient

Stores well – no fridge necessary

Packed in sachets – minimum waste

No mess

Often Complete

DRY FOOD *(Mixers and Meals, Biscuits, Vegetarian)*

Has most of the moisture taken out and may
contain only 10% water

Less expensive per unit of energy (weight for
weight)

Stores well - won't go off in dry, cool conditions

Convenient

Nutritious

More pleasant for Humans to handle

Vegetable protein less easy to digest

Available in bulk quantities

May be either Complete or Complementary

Some are less palatable - Canines have to learn to
like them

NB Dry foods work well with Canines because
they produce a lot of saliva, but ... **Always
ensure the diet contains sufficient fluid, with
drinking water freely available**.

THE SYMBOLS & ABBREVIATIONS WE USE
FOR MANUFACTURED DOG FOODS

FOOD TYPE

WET

MOIST/SEMI-MOIST

DRY

PACKAGING

TIN

BOX

FOIL

POT

PAPER SACK/WRAPPER

OTHER

AVAILABLE FROM

SUPERMARKET (S)

MINI-MARKET (M)

PET SHOP (P)

OTHER (O)
(e.g. Breeder, vet, garden centre, petrol station).

KEY TO
WET NOSE RATING

5 OUTSTANDING - A GASTRONOMIC DELIGHT

4 GOOD - DELICIOUS EATING

3 QUITE GOOD - TASTY EATING

2 VERY AVERAGE - BORING EATING

1 BELOW AVERAGE - ONLY EATEN WHEN DESPERATE

In addition to the Wet Nose Rating, a **'WAGGING TAIL'**

is awarded to dog foods of outstanding gastronomic interest - **RECOMMENDED EATING**

Dog Foods nominated for a Golden or Silver Nose Award (see pages 124–125) are marked with an asterisk *

FOOD REPORT NO. 1

BRAND NAME *Asda Supreme*

FLAVOUR *Beef & Heart*

PACKAGING

FOOD TYPE *Complementary*

MANUFACTURER *Asda Supermarkets*

PACK SIZE *1.18kg*

PURCHASED FROM (S) *Own label variety*

NOTES
*Should be fed with an equal volume of biscuit meal.
Asda's other wet food range is 'Quality' available in
395 and 765gms*

INSPECTOR *Cleo & Tasha*

INSPECTOR'S COMMENTS
This was a real tail wagger

WET NOSE RATING

SUPPLEMENTARY REPORTS
Asda Supreme: Lamb *Crackers* 3
Rabbit & Kidney *Duke* 3
Chicken *Cleo & Tasha* 5
Asda Quality: Chicken & Liver *Dougal* 5

HUMAN COMMENTS
Full of meat and went down a treat

Hey! Stop wagging!!

Tasha   Cleo

FOOD REPORT No. 2

BRAND NAME   *Asda Dog Mixer*

FLAVOUR   *Natural Whole Wheat*

PACKAGING

FOOD TYPE   *Complementary*

MANUFACTURER   *Asda Supermarkets*

PACK SIZE   *2.5kg*

PURCHASED FROM   Ⓢ *Own label variety*

NOTES
Should be fed with an equal volume of tinned food.
700gm size also available

INSPECTOR   *Bella*

INSPECTOR'S COMMENTS
Very sociable – a good mixer

WET NOSE RATING

SUPPLEMENTARY REPORTS
Asda Dog Meal: *Cleo & Tasha* 4

HUMAN COMMENTS
A well received own label mixer

FOOD REPORT NO. 3

BRAND NAME   *Bakers Complete*

FLAVOUR   *Beef*

PACKAGING

FOOD TYPE   *Complete*

MANUFACTURER   *Edward Baker*

PACK SIZE   *900gm*

PURCHASED FROM   (S) (M) (P) (O)

NOTES
*Also available in chicken flavour. Other sizes are
1.25kg, 2.5kg and 6kg. A similar product from the same
manufacturer is Omega Sally's Soft Minced Dog Food
in 4 × 150gm sachets.*

INSPECTOR   *Crackers*

INSPECTOR'S COMMENTS
*You can keep this on the menu, but don't forget the
water*

WET NOSE RATING[*]

SUPPLEMENTARY REPORTS
Beef: *Duke 3, Dougal 3, Bella 4*

HUMAN COMMENTS
*Good but expensive. Doesn't smell or attract flies in
hot weather*

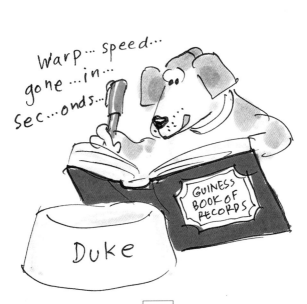

FOOD REPORT NO. 4

BRAND NAME   *Beta Chunks in Gravy*

FLAVOUR   *Chicken*

PACKAGING

FOOD TYPE   *Complementary*

MANUFACTURER   *Paragon Petcare*

PACK SIZE   *400gm*

PURCHASED FROM   (S) (P) (O)

NOTES
*Should be served with equal volume of biscuit mixer.
Other flavour 'Original'. Beta Dog Feast 400gm Wet
range includes Chicken & Rabbit; original Meat & Liver
flavours. Also available Beta Tripe Mix*

INSPECTOR   *Duke*

INSPECTOR'S COMMENTS
Designed for warp-speed consumption

WET NOSE RATING

SUPPLEMENTARY REPORTS
Beta Chunks: Chicken *Bella* 3, *Crackers* 4, *Cleo
& Tasha* 4
Beta Tripe Mix: *Piggy* 2

HUMAN COMMENTS
Woofed back in seconds

FOOD REPORT NO. 5

BRAND NAME *Beta Field*

FLAVOUR

PACKAGING

FOOD TYPE *Complete*

MANUFACTURER *Paragon Petcare*

PACK SIZE *2.5kg*

PURCHASED FROM (P) (O)

NOTES
*May be fed dry or moistened with water. Large range of
Complete dry foods available: Breeder; Puppy; Pet;
Racer; Recipe; Bravo; and Brutus. Biscuit mixers
include Digestive; Puppy; Terrier; Hound. Assorted:
Puppy; Terrier*

INSPECTOR *Dougal*

INSPECTOR'S COMMENTS
Digested of Tunbridge Wells

WET NOSE RATING

SUPPLEMENTARY REPORTS
Field: *Piggy* 3
Recipe: *Duke* 2

HUMAN COMMENTS
According to Dougal . . . quite tasty

FOOD REPORT NO. 6

BRAND NAME   *Bonus*

FLAVOUR   *Chicken & Liver*

PACKAGING

FOOD TYPE   *Complementary*

MANUFACTURER   *Spillers*

PACK SIZE   *800gm*

PURCHASED FROM   (S) (M) (P) (O)

NOTES
*Should be fed with an equal volume of mixer meal.
Recyclable tin. This range is available in various
flavours and sizes*

INSPECTOR   *Crackers*

INSPECTOR'S COMMENTS
Serious eating . . . too good for a chicken joke

WET NOSE RATING

SUPPLEMENTARY REPORTS
Chicken & Liver *Cleo & Tasha*
Rabbit *Cleo & Tasha* 4, *Crackers* 4
Original *Rambo* 3, *Cleo & Tasha* 4
Tuna & Chicken *Bella* 4
Beef & Kidney *Monty* 4, *Duke* 3
Tripe & Beef *Dougal* 4

HUMAN COMMENTS
*Crackers gave this bonus points for flavour
combination*

FOOD REPORT NO. 7

BRAND NAME   *Bounce Superchunks*

FLAVOUR   *Lamb & Turkey*

PACKAGING

FOOD TYPE   *Complementary*

MANUFACTURER   *Pedigree Petfoods*

PACK SIZE   *790gm*

PURCHASED FROM   (S) (M) (P) (O)

NOTES
Should be fed with an equal volume of mixer. Other flavours: Beef Superchunks; Beef & Poultry Superchunks; Liver Superchunks; Beef Original. Sizes range from 400–1650gm

---

INSPECTOR   *Bella*

INSPECTOR'S COMMENTS
Behind every Great Alsatian is a good dog food . . .

WET NOSE RATING   ϵϵϵϵ

SUPPLEMENTARY REPORTS
Superchunks: Beef *Rambo* 3, *Crackers* 4, *Dougal* 3,
    Lamb & Turkey *Duke* 3
    Cleo & Tasha 4
Beef Original: *Cleo & Tasha* 3

HUMAN COMMENTS
Sloppy texture but merited good marks

Good marks.

Bella

Class.

Buffet
à la carte

FOOD REPORT NO. 8

BRAND NAME   *Buffet a la Carte*

FLAVOUR   *Game*

PACKAGING

FOOD TYPE   *Complete*

MANUFACTURER   *Friskies Petcare*

PACK SIZE   *150gm*

PURCHASED FROM   (S) (M) (P) (O)

NOTES
*Other flavours: Beef; Lamb & Heart; Rabbit & Chicken;
Turkey. Buffet Tin range in 390 or 750gm available in
Beef, Chicken, and Lamb flavours. Friskies also produce
Marrow Meal in 2.5kg sacks*

INSPECTOR   *Duke*

INSPECTOR'S COMMENTS
A real touch of class

WET NOSE RATING

SUPPLEMENTARY REPORTS
Buffet a la Carte:
    Game *Monty* 4. *Crackers* 4
    Turkey *Cleo & Tasha* 3
Buffet (tin): Beef *Rambo* 4
    Lamb *Dougal* 4, *Piggy* 4, *Bella* 4, *Rambo* 3

HUMAN COMMENTS
*Easy to open packaging. Couldn't get Duke's nose out
of the bowl*

A dog hamburger.

went
down
well...

FOOD REPORT NO. 9

BRAND NAME *Butch*

FLAVOUR *Beef*

PACKAGING

FOOD TYPE *Complementary*

MANUFACTURER *Paragon Petcare*

PACK SIZE *400gm*

PURCHASED FROM (S) (M) (P) (O)

NOTES
Should be fed with an equal volume of biscuit meal.
Usually sold in a four pack. Meat & Liver, Chicken, and
Rabbit complete the flavours

INSPECTOR *Crackers*

INSPECTOR'S COMMENTS
Good enough for a dog burger

WET NOSE RATING

SUPPLEMENTARY REPORTS
Beef: *Cleo & Tasha* 3, *Dougal* 3, *Bella* 3
Meat & Liver: *Piggy* 2, *Dougal* 3, *Crackers* 4, *Rambo* 3,
    Bella 3
Rabbit: *Piggy* 2, *Dougal* 2, *Monty* 3
Chicken: *Cleo & Tasha* 3, *Rambo* 3, *Bella* 4, *Piggy* 4

HUMAN COMMENTS
This went down well

FOOD REPORT NO. 10

BRAND NAME *Cesar Select Menus*

FLAVOUR *Duck & Liver*

PACKAGING

FOOD TYPE *Complete*

MANUFACTURER *Pedigree Petfoods*

PACK SIZE *150gm*

PURCHASED FROM (S) (M) (P) (O)

NOTES
Other flavours: Turkey & Lamb; Rabbit & Heart
(150gm). Cesar (tins): available in Beef; Chicken;
Rabbit; Beef & Chicken; Rabbit & Turkey; Lamb &
Kidney; Liver & Beef. Sizes 185 and 390gm

INSPECTOR *Monty*

INSPECTOR'S COMMENTS
Good for the Officer's Mess

WET NOSE RATING

SUPPLEMENTARY REPORTS
Select Menus (foil pack): Duck & Liver *Duke* 4
Cesar (tins): Beef & Chicken *Duke* 5, *Piggy* 5*
   Chicken *Monty* 4
   Rabbit & Turkey *Crackers* 4

HUMAN COMMENTS
Monty wouldn't let the other troops near this one

FOOD REPORT NO. 11

BRAND NAME   *Champ*

FLAVOUR   *Beef & Liver*

PACKAGING

FOOD TYPE   *Complete*

MANUFACTURER   *Spillers*

PACK SIZE   *800gm*

PURCHASED FROM   (S) (M) (P) (O)

NOTES
Recyclable tin. Champ Mixer also available

INSPECTOR   *Duke*

INSPECTOR'S COMMENTS
Jaw smacking!!

WET NOSE RATING

SUPPLEMENTARY REPORTS
Beef & Liver *Dougal* 4

HUMAN COMMENTS
Dougal's tail took on a high gyration effect

A fussy **WHAT**?

FOOD REPORT NO. 12

BRAND NAME   *Chappie*

FLAVOUR   *Original*

PACKAGING

FOOD TYPE   *Complete*

MANUFACTURER   *Pedigree Petfoods*

PACK SIZE   *825gm*

PURCHASED FROM   (S) (M) (P) (O)

NOTES
Other flavours: Chicken, and Tripe. Various sizes and easy to open ring pull cans. This brand has been established for over 50 years

---

INSPECTOR   *Bella*

INSPECTOR'S COMMENTS
There's no dog food like an old dog food . . .

WET NOSE RATING

SUPPLEMENTARY REPORTS
Original *Cleo & Tasha* 3, *Duke* 3
Tripe *Dougal* 4, *Rambo* 3
Chicken *Dougal* 2, *Rambo* 3, *Piggy* 3

HUMAN COMMENTS
By Bella's standards this was tasty eating . . . she really is a fussy bitch!

FOOD REPORT NO. 13

BRAND NAME   *Choice Supreme*

FLAVOUR   *Beef & Liver*

PACKAGING

FOOD TYPE   *Complementary*

MANUFACTURER   *Spillers*

PACK SIZE   *390gm*

PURCHASED FROM   (S) (M) (P) (O)

NOTES
Should be fed mixed with an equal volume of mixer meal. Also available in 765gm and other flavours

---

INSPECTOR   *Dougal*

INSPECTOR'S COMMENTS
I was really bowled over by this one

WET NOSE RATING

SUPPLEMENTARY REPORTS
Beef & Liver *Bella* 4, *Duke* 3, *Rambo* 4
Original *Cleo & Tasha* 2
Rabbit *Crackers* 3

HUMAN COMMENTS
Dougal did his canine vacuum cleaner act on this one

It hit me for six...

FOOD REPORT NO. 14

BRAND NAME | *Chub Dinner*

FLAVOUR | *Chicken*

PACKAGING

FOOD TYPE | *Complementary*

MANUFACTURER | *Webbox*

PACK SIZE | *800gm*

PURCHASED FROM | Ⓢ Ⓟ Ⓞ

NOTES
Should be fed with an equal weight of mixer. Do not freeze. Other flavours: Beef; Rabbit and Ox Tripe. Similar products available from Forthglade, Davies, Pets Choice, Greenfields and Prosper de Mulder

---

INSPECTOR | *Rambo*

INSPECTOR'S COMMENTS
I'd rather eat this than guard it!

WET NOSE RATING

SUPPLEMENTARY REPORTS
Chicken *Cleo & Tasha* 4
Rabbit *Monty* 3
Beef *Piggy* 3
Ox Tripe *Crackers* 4

HUMAN COMMENTS
A tasty product, not exclusive to sausage dogs!

FOOD REPORT NO. 15

BRAND NAME   *Chum*

FLAVOUR   *Beef & Heart*

PACKAGING

FOOD TYPE   *Complete*

MANUFACTURER   *Pedigree Petfoods*

PACK SIZE   *400gm*

PURCHASED FROM   Ⓢ Ⓜ Ⓟ Ⓞ

NOTES
Several Chum flavours. Recyclable tin. Other ranges include: Tender Bites, and Select Cuts. Also Mixer, Small Bite Mixer and New Complete available in dry products.

INSPECTOR   *Rambo*

INSPECTOR'S COMMENTS
Definitely the best of Chums!

WET NOSE RATING

SUPPLEMENTARY REPORTS
Beef & Heart *Duke* 4   Rabbit *Cleo & Tasha* 4
Chicken & Tuna *Piggy* 4   Original *Cleo & Tasha* 3
Chopped Tripe *Crackers* 5
Lamb *Cleo & Tasha* 4   Chicken *Rambo* 3
Tender Bites: Liver & Turkey *Rambo* 2   Beef *Rambo* 5
Select Cuts: Beef & Poultry *Dougal* 3, *Bella* 3
    Chicken & Game *Cleo & Tasha* 3, *Rambo* 1
Chum Mixer (dry) *Duke* 3

HUMAN COMMENTS
He rushed through it like a tube train!

FOOD REPORT NO. 16

BRAND NAME   *Chunky*

FLAVOUR   *Turkey*

PACKAGING

FOOD TYPE   *Complete*

MANUFACTURER   *Quaker*

PACK SIZE   *1240gm*

PURCHASED FROM   (S) (M) (P) (O)

NOTES
Several flavours available. Other sizes 412gm and 814gm. Recyclable tin

---

INSPECTOR   *Crackers*

INSPECTOR'S COMMENTS
Paw lickin' good

WET NOSE RATING

SUPPLEMENTARY REPORTS
Beef *Crackers* 5, *Duke* 3, *Bella* 3, *Dougal* 3
Chicken *Cleo & Tasha* 4

HUMAN COMMENTS
Licked the bowl clean – saves washing up!

58

FOOD REPORT NO. 17

BRAND NAME   *Chunky Minced Morsels*

FLAVOUR   *Beef Plus Marrowbone*

PACKAGING   *4 sachets*

FOOD TYPE   *Complete*

MANUFACTURER   *Quaker*

PACK SIZE   *400gm – 4 × 100 sachets*

PURCHASED FROM   (S) (M) (P) (O)

NOTES
Other flavours available. Larger size 900gm

INSPECTOR   *Duke*

INSPECTOR'S COMMENTS
I like sachets . . . tins ain't what they used to be

WET NOSE RATING*

SUPPLEMENTARY REPORTS
Beef Plus Marrowbone *Dougal* 3, *Piggy* 3, *Bella* 4,
   Crackers 3

HUMAN COMMENTS
Easy no mess product

FOOD REPORT NO. 18

BRAND NAME *Co-op Meaty Dog Food*

FLAVOUR *Rabbit*

PACKAGING

FOOD TYPE *Complete*

MANUFACTURER *Co-op Supermarkets*

PACK SIZE *400gm*

PURCHASED FROM (S) *Own label variety*

NOTES
Also in Rabbit flavour. Other ranges include Supermeat (Wet) and Dog Meal

---

INSPECTOR *Piggy*

INSPECTOR'S COMMENTS
Well worth an encore

WET NOSE RATING

SUPPLEMENTARY REPORTS
Rabbit *Crackers* 2
Beef *Duke* 3
Dog Meal *Cleo & Tasha* 3

HUMAN COMMENTS
A real hit for a thespian

FOOD REPORT NO. 19

BRAND NAME   *Cycle Light*

FLAVOUR

PACKAGING

FOOD TYPE   *Complete*

MANUFACTURER   *Quaker*

PACK SIZE   *2kg*

PURCHASED FROM   (P) (O)

NOTES
Low in calories. Should not be fed to puppies, pregnant or nursing females or hardworking canines. Also available in Growth, Adult, and Senior varieties. In 200gm–10kg sizes

---

INSPECTOR   *Piggy*

INSPECTOR'S COMMENTS
The sweet smell of success, but don't forget the water

WET NOSE RATING

SUPPLEMENTARY REPORTS
Cycle Growth *Duke 3*

HUMAN COMMENTS
Piggy had trouble swallowing this until water was added

FOOD REPORT NO. 20

BRAND NAME   *Denes Healthmeal*

FLAVOUR   *Natural White Meat*

PACKAGING

FOOD TYPE   *Complete*

MANUFACTURER   *Denes Natural Petfood*

PACK SIZE   *400gm*

PURCHASED FROM   (S) (P) (M) (O)

NOTES
Other flavours include: Chicken & Tripe; Beef & Liver;
Chicken & Lamb; Rabbit & Chicken; Chicken, Beef &
Liver. No artificial flavours or colourings added

INSPECTOR   *Monty*

INSPECTOR'S COMMENTS
A tin a day keeps the vet away

WET NOSE RATING

SUPPLEMENTARY REPORTS
Chicken & Tripe *Monty* 4, *Piggy* 3
Chicken, Beef & Liver *Duke* 4, *Monty* 3

HUMAN COMMENTS
Good healthy eating for Monty

FOOD REPORT No. 21

BRAND NAME   *Eukanuba Premium*

FLAVOUR

PACKAGING

FOOD TYPE   *Complete*

MANUFACTURER   *The Iams Company*

PACK SIZE   *1kg*

PURCHASED FROM   (P) (O)

NOTES
Also available in Puppy, Junior, Regular, and Light. Sizes from 200gm to 15kg

---

INSPECTOR   *Piggy*

INSPECTOR'S COMMENTS
Pssst . . . good enough for the royal corgis

WET NOSE RATING*

SUPPLEMENTARY REPORTS
Premium *Cleo & Tasha* 5, *Rambo* 3, *Monty* 1
Light *Cleo & Tasha* 3, *Duke* 3, *Piggy* 5
Regular *Duke* 3, *Bella* 3, *Monty* 1

HUMAN COMMENTS
A widely used Complete dry food – but don't forget the liquid refreshment

FOOD REPORT NO. 22

BRAND NAME *Frolic*

FLAVOUR *Real Beef*

PACKAGING

FOOD TYPE *Complete*

MANUFACTURER *Pedigree Petfoods*

PACK SIZE *500gm*

PURCHASED FROM (S) (M) (P) (O)

NOTES
For other semi-moist products see Hi Life (Report No. 29); Chunky Minced Morsels (Report No 17) and Bakers Complete (Report No. 3)

INSPECTOR *Rambo*

INSPECTOR'S COMMENTS
Open the Box!

WET NOSE RATING *

SUPPLEMENTARY REPORTS
Beef *Duke 5, Crackers 4, Dougal 5*

HUMAN COMMENTS
An instant winner, being easy and convenient to use

And I mean NOW!

69

FOOD REPORT No. 23

BRAND NAME   *Gateway – Somerfield Supermeat*

FLAVOUR   *Liver*

PACKAGING

FOOD TYPE   *Complementary*

MANUFACTURER   *Gateway Foodmarkets*

PACK SIZE   *400gm*

PURCHASED FROM   (S)   *Own label variety*

NOTES
*Should be fed with an equal volume of meal or biscuit.
Other flavours: Chicken; Beef and Rabbit. Another
Somerfield range is Special Reserve, in various flavours*

INSPECTOR   *Duke*

INSPECTOR'S COMMENTS
Never say diet!

WET NOSE RATING

SUPPLEMENTARY REPORTS
Liver *Piggy* 4
Chicken *Bella* 4

HUMAN COMMENTS
Good jelly, good eating, and good value!

71

FOOD REPORT NO. 24

BRAND NAME   *Gilpa Valu*

FLAVOUR   *Meaty Chunks*

PACKAGING

FOOD TYPE   *Complete*

MANUFACTURER   *Gilbertson & Page*

PACK SIZE   *3kg*

PURCHASED FROM   (S) (M) (P) (O)

NOTES
Other sizes are 5, 10 and 20kg. Gilpa also produce Pup Complete in 10kg size and Imperial Complete in 800gm, 1.5kg and 2.5kg sizes. Free from artificial colours and flavourings

---

INSPECTOR   *Cleo & Tasha*

INSPECTOR'S COMMENTS
We swallowed this at double speed

WET NOSE RATING*

SUPPLEMENTARY REPORTS
Gilpa Valu *Dougal* 4, *Duke* 5 (Recommended)
   Crackers 5, *Bella* 5

HUMAN COMMENTS
They loved it

FOOD REPORT NO. 25

BRAND NAME   *Goldstar*

FLAVOUR   *Beef*

PACKAGING

FOOD TYPE   *Complementary*

MANUFACTURER   *Paragon Petcare*

PACK SIZE   *400gm*

PURCHASED FROM   (S) (M) (P) (O)

NOTES
*Should be served with equal volume of biscuit mixer –
purchased in a six pack*

INSPECTOR   *Rambo*

INSPECTOR'S COMMENTS
Very average – a real dog's dinner

WET NOSE RATING

SUPPLEMENTARY REPORTS
Beef *Piggy* 2, *Duke* 1

HUMAN COMMENTS
Rambo didn't shoot the place up over this one

FOOD REPORT NO. 26

BRAND NAME   *Goodlife*

FLAVOUR   *Beef & Lamb*

PACKAGING   *Ring pull plastic 'tin'*

FOOD TYPE    *Complementary*

MANUFACTURER   *Spillers*

PACK SIZE   *360gm*

PURCHASED FROM   (S) (M) (P) (O)

NOTES
*Should be fed mixed with an equal volume of mixer
meal. No artificial preservatives. Use within 24 hours of
opening. Other interesting flavours available*

INSPECTOR   *Monty*

INSPECTOR'S COMMENTS
This food is good enough to keep in the Dogger Bank

WET NOSE RATING*

SUPPLEMENTARY REPORTS
Beef & Lamb *Crackers* 5, *Duke* 5 (Recommended),
   Cleo & Tasha 3, *Piggy* 3
Beef & Turkey *Rambo* 3, *Dougal* 4, *Crackers* 5
Chicken & Liver *Bella* 5, *Monty* 5 (Recommended)

HUMAN COMMENTS
A five star rating from the General

FOOD REPORT No. 27

BRAND NAME   *Happidog*

FLAVOUR

PACKAGING

FOOD TYPE   *Complete*

MANUFACTURER   *Happidog Pet Foods*

PACK SIZE (GM)   *2kg*

PURCHASED FROM   Ⓟ Ⓞ

NOTES
*Other sizes include 10 and 20kg. Also available
Happidog Healthfood (Wet) in 400gm tins. Free from
artificial colourings and preservatives*

INSPECTOR   *Monty*

INSPECTOR'S COMMENTS
Only worth a short tour of duty

WET NOSE RATING

SUPPLEMENTARY REPORTS
Happidog Healthfood (Wet) *Duke* 3, *Piggy* 1

HUMAN COMMENTS
He only ate it because he was hungry

FOOD REPORT NO. 28

BRAND NAME   *Hardy Complete*

FLAVOUR   *Cereal, Meat, Fish and Vegetables*

PACKAGING   *Plastic*

FOOD TYPE   *Complete*

MANUFACTURER   *Companion Animal Foods*

PACK SIZE (GM)   *2.5kg*

PURCHASED FROM   Ⓢ Ⓜ Ⓟ Ⓞ

NOTES
Always ensure there is plenty of water. Sizes range from 800gm to 5kg. Hardy Junior available for Younger Canines

---

INSPECTOR   *Monty*

INSPECTOR'S COMMENTS
Yes . . . kiss me Hardy!

WET NOSE RATING*

SUPPLEMENTARY REPORTS
Duke 4, Crackers 5

HUMAN COMMENTS
Monty also liked it because it didn't fly through him like Concorde

FOOD REPORT NO. 29

BRAND NAME   *Hi Life Gourmet*

FLAVOUR   *Beef flavoured with*
                     Cheddar cheese

PACKAGING   *6 sachets*

FOOD TYPE   *Complete*

MANUFACTURER   *Town & Country Petfoods*

PACKSIZE   *900gm – 6 × 150gm sachets*

PURCHASED FROM   (S) (M) (P) (O)

NOTES
Recyclable packaging, small range with unusual
flavours

INSPECTOR   *Dougal*

INSPECTOR'S COMMENTS
Should have been a six!

WET NOSE RATING*

SUPPLEMENTARY REPORTS
Beef & Cheddar Cheese *Cleo & Tasha* 5,
   Piggy 5 (Recommended), *Duke* 5, *Bella* 4
Chicken & Tripe *Duke* 4, *Cleo & Tasha* 5 (Recommended)

HUMAN COMMENTS
Sounds like a cheese burger – but very convenient for
Dougal when he has an away match

FOOD REPORT NO. 30

BRAND NAME   *Hi Life Gourmet*

FLAVOUR   *Chicken with Selected*
                          Vegetables & Brown Rice

PACKAGING

FOOD TYPE   *Complete*

MANUFACTURER   *Town & Country Petfoods*

PACK SIZE   *400gm*

PURCHASED FROM   (S) (M) (P) (O)

NOTES
Especially good for Senior Canines with delicate
stomachs

INSPECTOR   *Cleo & Tasha*

INSPECTOR'S COMMENTS
A bird in the tin is worth two in the bush . . .

WET NOSE RATING*

SUPPLEMENTARY REPORTS
Beef *Crackers* 4, *Duke* 4
Chicken *Dougal* 5

HUMAN COMMENTS
An unusual flavour combination

85

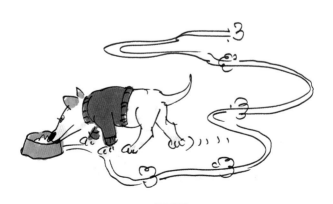

FOOD REPORT NO. 31

BRAND NAME   *Hill's Science Diet*

FLAVOUR   *Canine Maintenance*

PACKAGING

FOOD TYPE   *Complete*

MANUFACTURER   *Hill's*

PACK SIZE   *440gm*

PURCHASED FROM

NOTES
Science Diets are available in both wet and dry form.
The range also includes Maintenance Light; Growth;
Performance; Senior and Prescription diets. (Specific
medical problems under the supervision of a Vet)

INSPECTOR   *Piggy*

INSPECTOR'S COMMENTS
This almost brought the house down

WET NOSE RATING

SUPPLEMENTARY REPORTS
Hill's Canine Performance (Wet) *Duke* 2
Hill's Maintenance (Dry) *Monty* 3, *Piggy* 5*,

HUMAN COMMENTS
Good but expensive and only obtainable from Vets.
Piggy pushed the bowl all round the kitchen till he
emptied it

clunk!

Ate without deviations...

FOOD REPORT NO. 32

BRAND NAME   *Kennomeat*

FLAVOUR   *Original*

PACKAGING

FOOD TYPE   *Complementary*

MANUFACTURER   *Spillers*

PACK SIZE   *390gm*

PURCHASED FROM   (S) (M) (P) (O)

NOTES
Should be fed with an equal volume of mixer meal.
Other sizes and flavours available

INSPECTOR   *Dougal*

INSPECTOR'S COMMENTS
A beautiful four

WET NOSE RATING

SUPPLEMENTARY REPORTS
Original *Bella* 4, *Crackers* 3, *Duke* 5
Rabbit *Duke* 5 (Recommended)

HUMAN COMMENTS
Ate without hesitation, deviation or . . .

FOOD REPORT No. 33

BRAND NAME	*Kibbles and Chunks*
FLAVOUR	*Whole Grain & Beefy Chunks*
PACKAGING	
FOOD TYPE	*Complete*
MANUFACTURER	*Purina*
PACK SIZE	*1.18kg*
PURCHASED FROM	(S) (M) (P) (O)

NOTES
Mixture of crunchy biscuits and chewy moist chunks. Also available in 3kg

---

INSPECTOR *Rambo*

INSPECTOR'S COMMENTS
A legend in its own crunch time

WET NOSE RATING

SUPPLEMENTARY REPORTS
Bella 4, Duke 4, Piggy 4

HUMAN COMMENTS
Rambo loved it, but the list of ingredients looked like a chemistry set!

FOOD REPORT NO. 34

BRAND NAME   *Marks & Spencer*
                     St Michael's Own Choice

FLAVOUR   *Chicken &*
                     Liver/Rabbit/Beef

PACKAGING

FOOD TYPE   *Complete*

MANUFACTURER   *Marks & Spencer*

PACK SIZE   *6 × 200gm*

PURCHASED FROM   (S) *Own label variety*

NOTES
High energy product. Three flavours in a box of six foils which resemble human choc ices. (Two new ranges available since our testings)

INSPECTOR   *Cleo & Tasha*

INSPECTOR'S COMMENTS
This was so good we put on our best dog collars for the occasion

WET NOSE RATING

SUPPLEMENTARY REPORTS
Chicken & Liver/Rabbit/Beef *Crackers* 5, *Duke* 5

HUMAN COMMENTS
They ate it faster than a speeding bullet . . .

FOOD REPORT NO. 35

BRAND NAME *Marks & Spencer*
St Michael's Own Choice

FLAVOUR *Beef & Heart*

PACKAGING

FOOD TYPE *Complementary*

MANUFACTURER *Marks & Spencer*

PACK SIZE *390gm*

PURCHASED FROM (S) *Own label variety*

NOTES
Should be fed with an equal volume of mixer meal.
Other flavours: Beef & Chicken; Beef. No artificial
additives. Also available: Own Choice Wholegrain
mixer meal in 1.5kg sacks

INSPECTOR *Crackers*

INSPECTOR'S COMMENTS
The way to a dog's stomach is through his beef and
heart . . .

WET NOSE RATING

SUPPLEMENTARY REPORTS
Beef *Rambo* 4, *Monty* 4
Beef & Chicken *Piggy* 4

HUMAN COMMENTS
This was a good dog food as dog foods go, and as dog
foods go, this went . . . fast!!

FOOD REPORT NO. 36

BRAND NAME *Midland Butcher's Tripe*

FLAVOUR *Tripe & Beef*

PACKAGING

FOOD TYPE *Complementary*

MANUFACTURER *Midland Petfood Canners*

PACK SIZE *390gm*

PURCHASED FROM Ⓢ Ⓜ Ⓟ Ⓞ

NOTES
*Should be fed with an equal volume of biscuit or meal.
Other flavours in range: Tripe Mix; Tripe & Liver;
Tripe & Chicken. Sizes from 185gm to 800gm. No
flavourings, colourings or preservatives*

INSPECTOR *Monty*

INSPECTOR'S COMMENTS
Caviar for the General

WET NOSE RATING*

*High rating confirmed by Duke, Cleo & Tasha, Dougal,
Bella, Rambo and Piggy*

SUPPLEMENTARY REPORTS
Tripe & Chicken *Cleo & Tasha* 5, *Monty* 5 (Recommended)
Tripe Mix *Piggy* 3, *Monty* 5, *Crackers* 3, *Cleo & Tasha* 4

HUMAN COMMENTS
A 21 gum salute from Monty

FOOD REPORT No. 37

BRAND NAME   *Pal*

FLAVOUR   *Rabbit*

PACKAGING

FOOD TYPE   *Complementary*

MANUFACTURER   *Pedigree*

PACK SIZE   *390gm*

PURCHASED FROM   (S) (M) (P) (O)

NOTES
Should be served with an equal volume of mixer. Other ranges are Pal Partners and Pal Partners Lite – in an interesting variety of flavours, with sizes up to 1200gm

---

INSPECTOR   *Crackers*

INSPECTOR'S COMMENTS
. . . Paws for thought

WET NOSE RATING

SUPPLEMENTARY REPORTS
Rabbit *Duke* 5, *Dougal* 3, *Piggy* 3, *Bella* 4,
     Cleo & Tasha 3
Beef *Duke* 4, *Piggy* 3
Partners Lite: Turkey & Carrots *Cleo & Tasha* 5 + Rec
Partners: Beef & Liver *Cleo & Tasha* 4, Turkey & Liver
     Rambo 2, *Piggy* 2

HUMAN COMMENTS
. . . Food for thought

FOOD REPORT NO. 38

BRAND NAME　　　　　*Prime*

FLAVOUR　　　　　*Tripe*

PACKAGING

FOOD TYPE　　　　　*Complementary*

MANUFACTURER　　　*Spillers*

PACK SIZE　　　　*400gm*

PURCHASED FROM　　 S M P O

NOTES
*Should be fed with an equal volume of mixer. Several
other flavours available in sizes up to 1200gm.
Recyclable tin*

INSPECTOR　　　　*Cleo & Tasha*

INSPECTOR'S COMMENTS
Was it good for you two?

WET NOSE RATING

SUPPLEMENTARY REPORTS
Tripe *Duke* 3
Chicken & Liver *Cleo & Tasha* 4, *Crackers* 4
Lamb *Rambo* 3, *Piggy* 3
Turkey *Duke* 3, *Rambo* 4
Rabbit *Monty* 3　　Original *Crackers* 3
Beef & Kidney *Dougal* 4, *Bella* 2

HUMAN COMMENTS
Sloppy, but good

FOOD REPORT NO. 39

BRAND NAME   *Repnor Gold*

FLAVOUR   *Original*

PACKAGING

FOOD TYPE   *Complete*

MANUFACTURER   *Repnor Gold Products*

PACK SIZE   *2.5kg*

PURCHASED FROM   (P) (O)

NOTES
Other ranges include: Puppy Gold; Racing Gold; and Supreme Gold. In sizes from 2.5kg to 20kg

---

INSPECTOR   *Duke*

INSPECTOR'S COMMENTS
Quite good, though not worth breaking into the cupboard for it

WET NOSE RATING

SUPPLEMENTARY REPORTS
Original *Cleo & Tasha* 3
Racing Gold *Piggy* 3

HUMAN COMMENTS
Duke had problems swallowing this even with a little water

FOOD REPORT No. 40

BRAND NAME   *Safeway Dog Meal*

FLAVOUR

PACKAGING

FOOD TYPE   *Complementary*

MANUFACTURER   *Safeway Supermarkets*

PACK SIZE   *800gm*

PURCHASED FROM   (S) *Own label variety*

NOTES
May be fed dry or soaked in gravy, milk or water and mixed with wet food. Additional sizes 3kg and 5kg. Other Safeway Dry products include: Dog Biscuits and Bones; and Mixermeal

---

INSPECTOR   *Dougal*

INSPECTOR'S COMMENTS
Howzat . . . a fair catch

WET NOSE RATING

SUPPLEMENTARY REPORTS
Dog Meal *Cleo & Tasha* 3
Dog Biscuits *Duke* 5, *Bella* 4

HUMAN COMMENTS
A good average crunch

FOOD REPORT NO. 41

BRAND NAME   *Safeway Reward*

FLAVOUR   *Rabbit*

PACKAGING

FOOD TYPE   *Complementary*

MANUFACTURER   *Safeway Supermarkets*

PACK SIZE   *400gm*

PURCHASED FROM   Ⓢ *Own label variety*

NOTES
*Should be fed with an equal weight of mixer meal.
Other Safeway ranges include Premium; Prime Cuts;
and 'Dog Food' – in several flavours and sizes*

INSPECTOR   *Cleo & Tasha*

INSPECTOR'S COMMENTS
This deserves the nobel prize for food!

WET NOSE RATING

SUPPLEMENTARY REPORTS
Reward: Rabbit *Crackers* 5 (Recommended)
   Original *Duke* 3
   Chicken *Bella* 5
Prime Cuts: Rabbit *Crackers* 3
   Chicken *Piggy* 3, *Cleo & Tasha* 4
   Lamb *Monty* 4
   Beef *Dougal* 4
'Dog Food': Meat Recipe *Rambo* 3

HUMAN COMMENTS
A most rewarding product

FOOD REPORT NO. 42

BRAND NAME   *Sainsbury Tripe Mix*

FLAVOUR   *Tripe Mix*

PACKAGING

FOOD TYPE   *Complementary*

MANUFACTURER   *Sainsbury Supermarkets*

PACK SIZE   *815gm*

PURCHASED FROM   (S) *Own label variety*

NOTES
*Feed with an equal volume of quality mixer or meal.
Contains no soya or cereal. Other Sainsbury's ranges
in several flavours and sizes: Supermeat; Supreme;
Supreme Selection; and Gourmet Selection and
Chunks.*

INSPECTOR   *Bella*

INSPECTOR'S COMMENTS
The only way to remove temptation is to yield to it

WET NOSE RATING

SUPPLEMENTARY REPORTS
(Representative of over 50 testings from the 6 ranges)
Tripe Mix *Dougal* 5   Tripe Mix & Lamb *Crackers* 4
Gourmet Chunks: Beef, Tripe & Vegetables *Bella* 5
    Chicken & Turkey *Monty* 4
Gourmet selection: Beef & Chicken *Rambo* 3
Supermeat: Beef & Chicken *Piggy* 4
Supreme: Duck, Heart & Kidney *Crackers* 5
Supreme Selection: Turkey & Venison *Bella* 4

HUMAN COMMENTS
A very good own label variety

FOOD REPORT NO. 43

BRAND NAME   *Sainsbury Supreme Mixer*

FLAVOUR   *Wholemeal*

PACKAGING

FOOD TYPE   *Complementary*

MANUFACTURER   *Sainsbury Supermarkets*

PACK SIZE   *1kg*

PURCHASED FROM   (S) *Own label variety*

NOTES
Vitamin enriched. Should be mixed with the appropriate quantity of canned dog food. Other products in Sainsbury's Dry range include: Mixameal Dog Meal; Krunchies; and Biscuits – in sizes from 500gm

---

INSPECTOR   *Monty*

INSPECTOR'S COMMENTS
Only obeying orders . . . but not at all bad

WET NOSE RATING

SUPPLEMENTARY REPORTS
Mixameal *Cleo & Tasha* 3, *Terry* 3
Dog Biscuits *Dougal* 1
Krunchies *Rambo* 2

HUMAN COMMENTS
A good meal, but not Monty's favourite

FOOD REPORT NO. 44

BRAND NAME   *Tesco Complete Dog Food*

FLAVOUR   *Mixed Cereal and Meat*

PACKAGING

FOOD TYPE   *Complete*

MANUFACTURER   *Tesco Supermarkets*

PACK SIZE   *3kg*

PURCHASED FROM   (S) *Own label variety*

NOTES
*Tesco Dry ranges also include: Dog Meal; Dog Mixer;
and Small Bite Mixer. Sizes from 500gm to 5kg. No
artificial colours, flavourings or preservatives*

INSPECTOR   *Rambo*

INSPECTOR'S COMMENTS
Worth doubling the guard for!

WET NOSE RATING

SUPPLEMENTARY REPORTS
Dog Meal *Cleo & Tasha* 3
Dog Mixer *Duke* 2

HUMAN COMMENTS
Makes a change from tins

If it's worth doing...

FOOD REPORT No. 45

BRAND NAME   *Tesco Meaty Chunks*

FLAVOUR   *Turkey & Chicken*

PACKAGING

FOOD TYPE   *Complementary*

MANUFACTURER   *Tesco Supermarkets*

PACK SIZE   *780gm*

PURCHASED FROM   (S) *Own label variety*

NOTES
*Recyclable steel tin. Should be fed mixed with an equal
volume of dog meal. Other Tesco Wet ranges include
Feast, and Premium, in several flavours and sizes*

INSPECTOR   *Piggy*

INSPECTOR'S COMMENTS
If a tin is worth doing it's worth doing well!

WET NOSE RATING

SUPPLEMENTARY REPORTS
Beef & Tripe *Cleo & Tasha* 4, *Dougal* 5
Rabbit *Dougal* 2, *Cleo & Tasha* 4, *Bella* 2, *Piggy* 4
Turkey & Chicken *Bella* 3, *Dougal* 3
Lamb & Kidney *Bella* 3, *Dougal* 4
Premium: Chicken *Rambo* 3
   Chicken & Rabbit *Cleo & Tasha* 5 (Recommended),
   Dougal 4
Feast: Beef & Kidney *Bella* 3
   Lamb & Kidney *Rambo* 3

HUMAN COMMENTS
Piggy felt this deserved good marks from the critics

FOOD REPORT NO. 46

BRAND NAME   *Wafcol*

FLAVOUR   *Vegetarian*

PACKAGING

FOOD TYPE   *Complete*

MANUFACTURER   *Wafcol*

PACK SIZE   *5kg*

PURCHASED FROM   (S) (P) (O)

NOTES
*Part of the extensive Wafcol range e.g. 24 Active
Betterflakes; Racing; and Bonemeal. See under
Auxiliary Inspectors for other Wafcol products*

INSPECTOR   *Dougal*

INSPECTOR'S COMMENTS
*This food suffers from the boredom of nutritional
excellence*

WET NOSE RATING

SUPPLEMENTARY REPORTS
Special 21 *Rambo* 2

HUMAN COMMENTS
After 'Tea' Dougal fell asleep in the pavilion

113

FOOD REPORT No. 47

BRAND NAME   *Waitrose Special Recipe*

FLAVOUR   *Rabbit, Game & Vegetables*

PACKAGING

FOOD TYPE   *Complete*

MANUFACTURER   *Waitrose Supermarkets*

PACK SIZE   *1.25kg*

PURCHASED FROM   (S) *Own label variety*

NOTES
Unnecessary to supplement with mixer. Other flavours include: Beef & Vegetables; Chicken & Tripe with Green Vegetables & Pasta – in sizes from 800gm to 1.25kg. Also Special Recipe for Small Dogs in interesting flavour combinations

---

INSPECTOR   *Piggy*

INSPECTOR'S COMMENTS
This one will run and run . . .

WET NOSE RATING

SUPPLEMENTARY REPORTS
Beef & Vegetables *Rambo* 2, *Monty* 1
Chicken & Tripe with Green Vegetables & Pasta *Cleo*
      & Tasha 4
Rabbit, Game & Vegetables *Dougal* 4
Special Recipe for Small Dogs: Tripe, Turkey & Carrots
      Duke 4

HUMAN COMMENTS
Never knowingly undereaten!

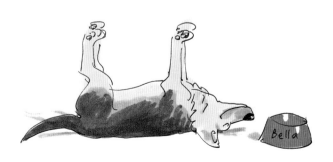

FOOD REPORT NO. 48

BRAND NAME   *Winalot*

FLAVOUR   *Wholegrain*

PACKAGING

FOOD TYPE   *Complementary*

MANUFACTURER   *Spillers*

PACK SIZE   *700gm*

PURCHASED FROM   (S) (M) (P) (O)

NOTES
*Should be mixed with an equal volume of premium
canned food. The range also includes Mini Winalot,
and Traditional Wholewheat, in sizes from 500gm to
20kg*

INSPECTOR   *Bella*

INSPECTOR'S COMMENTS
*Quite tasty . . . but, when I want your opinion I'll give
it to you*

WET NOSE RATING

SUPPLEMENTARY REPORTS
Mini Winalot *Cleo & Tasha* 5 (Recommended)
Wholegrain *Monty* 1, *Duke* 4

HUMAN COMMENTS
Bella showed no emotion

SPECIALIST FOOD TESTINGS
BY OUR
AUXILIARY INSPECTORS

BENJI *Senior/Less Active Food Specialist*

TESTINGS	RATING
Cycle Senior – Dry	3
Royal Canin – LA23 Dry	3

ALSO SUGGESTED:
Hill's Science Diet – Canine Senior
Liquivite
Pedigree Chappie – Original
Wafcol Veteran

BENSON JR. *Puppy/Junior/Growth Food Specialist*

TESTINGS	RATING
Elite Omega Puppy	4
Eukanuba Puppy	3
Hardy Complete – Junior	3
Cycle Growth	4

ALSO SUGGESTED:
Beta Puppy
Denes Nature Puppy
Febo Dry Puppy Food
Gilpa Pup
Hill's Canine Growth
Omega Dry Puppy Food
Pedigree Chum Puppy Food
Repnor Puppy Gold
Spillers Dog Diet I (puppy & small dog)
Wafcol Puppy Food
Winalot Puppy

SPECIALIST FOOD TESTINGS

TAMMY *Dry Food Specialist*

TESTINGS	RATING
Royal Canin M25 Maintenance	3
Febo Professional Gold Plus	4
Hill's Science Diet Maintenance	5 (Rec.)
Omega Tasty	3
Budgens Dog Meal	4

ALSO SUGGESTED:
Beta
Cycle
Febo
Friskie's Go-Dog
Eukanuba
Omega Elite Adult

GEMMA *'Limited Editions' Specialist*
(See note to explain 'Limited Editions' on page 17)

TESTINGS	RATING
Husky Meaty Dog Food	4
Jessie – Chicken	4
Jessie – Lamb	4
Morrisons Own Label Premium – Beef & Heart	4
Nisa Dog Food Rabbit	5
Red Heart Meat	2
Tex Chunks – Rabbit	4
Vetrabond Tripe Mix	4

SPECIALIST FOOD TESTINGS

TERRY *'Limited Editions' Specialist*

TESTINGS	RATING
Jessie – Tripe	3
Master's Choice Dog Food	3
Nisa Right Price – Meat & Cereal	3
Rufus – Chicken	3
Safari – Beef & Lamb	5
Tex Chunks – Chicken & Tripe	5 (Rec.)

DAISY *Health Food Specialist*
(Including Medical and Vegetarian Products both wet and dry)

TESTING	RATING
Happidog Complete – Dry	2
Happidog Healthfood – Wet	3
Wafcol Special 21 – Dry	1
Wafcol Vegetarian – Dry	3

ALSO SUGGESTED:
Cycle Light
Denes Natural Petfoods
Eukanuba Light
Hill's Science Diet Maintenance Light
Wafcol Rite-Weight

MEDICAL RANGES AVAILABLE:
(Only on prescription from vets and must be fed in accordance with their instructions)
Hill's Prescription Diet
Waltham Diet

CHEWS, CHOMPS, SNACKS & BISCUITS . . .

Chews... Chomps... Choc drops... Treats...

Biscuits... Bones... sticks... wot a life !!

There is an amazing choice to whet your appetite. The following are just some of our finds.

Chews - in rawhide came in a variety of shapes and sizes including shoes, rings, knuckles, shins and knotted bones; all good for exercising the bite and sharpening the 'canines' and it definitely beats a visit to the dentist.

Snacks - where to start is the problem. Pedigree produce a wide selection including Schmackos, Rodeo Strips, Dogstix and Dog Treats in such jaw-smacking flavours as liver, beef, and rabbit. Tandem are tender morsels that can be enjoyed in two flavours. Omega Poppalongs offered a similar style of sticks in a variety of flavours that also went down very well.

Treats - Good Boy have an enormous selection of goodies on offer for the 'sweet toothed' Canine, including Choc Drops, Jolly Drops, Large and Small Choc Bones, Sticks, Skippers and Meaty Bites. Trix chocolate-covered doughnuts and Treats in original, or chicken and beef, were another delight to the team. Oh, we almost forgot Snack Bones and Krunch. For those Canines that prefer white chocolate there are always the Milk Drops to try.

Wafcol and Binzo gave us more indulgences and we tracked down Doggy Mixtures, Snaffles, Krunchy Dog Chocs and Joy Sticks (great as a breath freshner) as well as Bones in plain, charcoal and chocolate flavours. Finally, Health Bars and Nutty Doughnuts complete this selection.

What a choice – but watch you don't overdo the chocolate.

Biscuits – if you thought the chews and snacks were mouthwatering, look what we found in the Biscuit ranges. Naturally, preferences varied from Inspector to Inspector, but the quality and choices available from the various manufacturers were all good and will never leave you hungry or bored.

The Beta brand offers Champion Nuckles (for Canines who can't spell), Mini-Bones, Fivers, Charcoal and New Scrunchies biscuits to mix with our other foods or to eat separately. Spillers selection included Bonio in original, beef, charcoal, marrowbone, and rabbit flavours. Mini Bonios, Mini Chops and Mixed Ovals were all readily available in several flavours and received high praise from the Inspectors. However, we mustn't leave out such old favourites as Spillers Shapes, Mixer, or newer products such as cheesy-tasting Crunchies or Marrowbone Cupids.

Other wholesome offerings from Pedigree include Bisrok Snacks, in Digestive, Mixed, and Crunchy Beef, which the manufacturer claims reduces the build up of plaque associated with Canine halitosis and dental problems. Original Markies and Mini-Markies in assorted tasty flavours were also rapidly vapourised.

Denes Mixer Biscuits, Nature Bite, Nature Treat and Nature Logs in Wholegrain gave our health-conscious canines an excellent selection. Davis offered Dog-E-Bisk and Pup-E-Bisk. Also from Pets Choice we have new Charcoal Chips. We tried Febo Professional Biscuits, Giant Biscuit Bones, Doggie Dominoes and Laughing Dog Milkwheat Biscuits. The Friskies range included Buffet Savoury Tubes in cheese and meat flavours, as well as cocoa-tasting Hearts and Crunchy Rings.

The major supermarkets generally had good selections of own label biscuits, bones and rolls, so get your human to buy them for a change.

All this should give you lots of ideas to get your teeth into, so why not **be adventurous** and try them all.

Try them all...

THE GOOD DOG FOOD
GUIDE AWARDS

*Silver Nose Award for the
Best Dry Dog Food*

NOMINEES
Eukanuba – Premium
Hardy Complete
Hill's Science Maintenance Diet
Gilpa Valu
Winner: Gilpa Valu

*Silver Nose Award for the
Best Wet Dog Food*

NOMINEES
Midland Butcher's Tripe – Tripe & Beef
Spillers Goodlife – Beef & Lamb
Hi Life Gourmet – Chicken with Selected
Vegetables & Brown Rice
Pedigree Petfoods Cesar – Beef & Chicken

**Winner: Midland Butcher's
Tripe – Tripe & Beef**

*Silver Nose Award for the
Best Moist/Semi-moist Dog Food*

NOMINEES
Pedigree Frolic – Beef
Quaker Chunky Minced Morsels – Beef
Bakers Complete – Beef
Hi Life Gourmet – Beef Flavoured with Cheddar
Cheese

**Winner: Hi Life Gourmet
Beef Flavoured with Cheddar
Cheese**

THE GOLDEN NOSE AWARD
FOR THE
BEST DOG FOOD OF 1993

**WINNER: MIDLAND BUTCHER'S
TRIPE – TRIPE & BEEF**

A LAST WORD FROM THE CHIEF INSPECTOR

Phewwwwwww ... that was a lot of eating.
Between us – eight full-time and six Auxiliary Inspectors – we have chewed, chomped, gnawed and yawned our way through over 450 different brands, varieties and flavours of Dog Food.

The range of products now available to adventurous eaters is excellent and growing all the time. The manufacturers have become more inventive and are not just producing the same boring stuff we've had for years. There are now some really interesting combinations to wrap our canines round.

We tried all sorts of new foods, with tasty ingredients such as rice, vegetables and pastas. These proved welcome additions to old favourites and made eating more exciting. We all now look forward to mealtimes with added relish.

Some of the wet foods served on their own caused severe 'bathroom' problems and were only tolerated for the sake of the Guide – over and above the call of duty. Others were much improved when either mixer or meal was added. We do wish that Humans would read the labels more often.

Are you going to be long?!

BATHROOM

Rambo, alas, had to resign his commission when his owner decided that a particular semi-moist product was more convenient for him because it was easy to open, serve and caused no mess. As an Inspector he is bitterly disappointed that he has to eat the same thing every day and can no longer pursue the cause of adventurous eating.

One complaint made by several of the team was that only 'nice' doggies who don't growl or show their canines are pictured on the packaging, never macho dogs like Great Danes or British Bull Dogs . . . grrrrrr.

The majority of Inspectors feel that the manufacturers have almost got it right and with a little more consultation, dinner times will have a five nose rating every day . . . but we wouldn't want to be dogmatic.

But I was _born_ for adventure!